THE FINANCE (No 2) ACT 1983

Contributors
D. W. BOND, ATII, Solicitor
Z. KRONBERGS, BSc, ARCS, ACA
S. A. PARRINGTON, LLB
R. A. WALLINGTON, MA, Barrister
G. WIGNALL, LLB

LONDON
BUTTERWORTHS
1983

ISBN 0 406 08056 9

Printed and bound in Great Britain by The Whitefriars Press Ltd., Tonbridge

RELEVANT DATES

1983	
25 May	Publication of Finance Bill
26 July	Royal Assent

CONTENTS

INTRODUCTION

This is the second Finance Act of 1983. The first, FA 1983 (see separate booklet), received Royal Assent on 13 May 1983. Parliament was dissolved on that date and a general election was held on 9 June 1983. Several provisions which had been proposed in the Finance Bill before the election had to be deleted from that Bill to ensure its passage through the House of Commons. A few of these have been included in F(No 2)A 1983; it is expected that others will reappear in the 1984 Finance Bill.

INCOME TAX, CORPORATION TAX AND CAPITAL GAINS TAX

Income tax rate bands and thresholds The income tax basic rate limit, higher rate bands and investment income threshold are increased to the amounts originally proposed in the Budget Resolutions passed on 21 March 1983 but not enacted in FA 1983 (s 1).

Small companies rate For the financial year 1982 the lower rate of corporation tax applies to the income of companies whose profits do not exceed £100,000 with marginal relief where profits exceed this but do not exceed £500,000 (s 2). The small companies rate was reduced to 38 per cent by FA 1983 s 13.

Interest relief limit The limit on the amount of home loans for which interest relief is available is increased to £30,000 for 1983–84. The corresponding limit in respect of secured loans for the purchase of life annuities is also increased to £30,000 (s 3).

Beneficial loans and the interest relief limit The benefit to the employee from an interest-free loan by his employer is exempt from tax insofar as relief would have been available to the borrower if interest had been payable on that loan. From 1983–84 an interest-free loan by an employer is treated as made after any interest-bearing loan eligible for relief to which the £30,000 limit applies. The notional relief for the employee in respect of the benefit of the interest-free loan will therefore be restricted to the balance, if any, of the £30,000 limit after deducting the total amount of all loans on which interest is payable and eligible for relief (s 4).

Business expansion scheme FA 1983 s 26, Sch 5 introduced a scheme to provide for income tax relief for sums invested in subscribing for ordinary shares in certain unquoted trading companies. The scheme is broadly based on the earlier Business Start-up Scheme which applied for 1981–82 and 1982–83. Amendments are made to the provisions of FA 1983 Sch 5 to correct perceived technical defects (s 5, Sch 1).

Dwellinghouses let on assured tenancies FA 1982 Sch 12 provided for capital allowances to be available for expenditure on the construction of buildings as, or including, dwelling-houses let on assured tenancies. Two technical amendments are made to the provisions of that Schedule and the capital allowances are restricted to those approved bodies which are companies (s 6).

Boundary changes in parliamentary constituencies Where property is transferred from one local constituency association to another following a change in constituency boundaries, relief is provided in respect of the capital gains tax (s 7) and stamp duty (s 15) liability to which the transfer might otherwise give rise. The new reliefs are available in respect of the boundary changes which took effect in 1983 and any subsequent changes.

CAPITAL TRANSFER TAX

Rates of capital transfer tax The tables of rates originally proposed in the Budget Resolutions passed on 21 March 1983 but not included in FA 1983 are now enacted. The new rates apply to chargeable transfers made after 14 March 1983. Accordingly, the CTT (Indexation) Order 1983 (SI 1983/403) has no effect (s 8).

Gifts to charities The exemption limit of £250,000 in respect of gifts and bequests to charities made on, or within one year before, the death of the transferor is abolished (s 9).

Business and agricultural property relief The rate of business property relief available in respect of the transfer of a minority shareholding in an unquoted company is increased to 30 per cent. The lower rate of agricultural property relief is also increased to 30 per cent (s 10).

Payment of tax by instalments Capital transfer tax which is attributable to business property, controlling shareholdings, certain minority unquoted shareholdings, land, or timber may be paid by instalments if certain conditions are fulfilled. The instalment period is increased to ten years and payments must be made annually. There is no longer an option for payment by half-yearly instalments (s 11).

Domicile The special rule for determining the domicile for capital transfer tax purposes of emigrants from the UK to the Channel Islands and the Isle of Man is abolished (s 12).

Burden of tax To resolve the uncertainty caused by the decision in *Re Dougal* [1981] STC 514, it is provided that capital transfer tax on realty is to be treated as a testamentary expense payable out of the residue of the estate of the deceased instead of being borne by the beneficiary of the property in question. This applies only in respect of deaths occurring after the passing of this Act where no contrary intention was expressed by the deceased in his will (s 13).

MISCELLANEOUS

Development land tax Certain operations in connection with the installation of advanced telecommunication systems are exempted from development land tax (s 14).

Stamp duty Exemption from stamp duty is provided for transfers of property between local constituency associations following changes in constituency boundaries (s 15).

THE FINANCE (No 2) ACT 1983

ARRANGEMENT OF SECTIONS

Part I

Income Tax, Corporation Tax and Capital Gains Tax

Part II

Capital Transfer Tax

Part III

Miscellaneous and Supplementary

Schedules:

An Act to grant certain duties, to alter other duties, and to amend the law relating to the National Debt and the Public Revenue, and to make further provision in connection with Finance.

[26 July 1983]

PART I

INCOME TAX, CORPORATION TAX AND CAPITAL GAINS TAX

1 Basic rate limit, higher rate bands and investment income threshold

For the year 1983–84 income tax shall be charged—

(*a*) in respect of so much of an individual's total income as exceeds £14,600 at such higher rates as are specified in the Table below; and

(*b*) in respect of so much of the investment income included in an individual's total income as exceeds £7,100 at the additional rate of 15 per cent.

TABLE

Part of excess over £14,600	*Higher rate*
The first £2,600	40 per cent
The next £4,600	45 per cent
The next £7,100	50 per cent
The next £7,100	55 per cent
The remainder	60 per cent;

and subsection (1) of section 32 of the Finance Act 1971 (charge of income tax) shall have effect accordingly.

GENERAL NOTE

This section reintroduces the rate bands and additional rate threshold originally proposed in Resolution 12 of the March 1983 Budget Resolutions.

The basic rate of 30 per cent (set by FA 1983 s 10 (1)) applies to total income not exceeding £14,600. The higher rates of tax which apply to income over £14,600 are set out in a table.

The additional rate threshold is increased from £6,250 to £7,100 but the single additional rate of 15 per cent is unchanged.

PAYE

Before the enactment of FA 1983, the Revenue issued revised PAYE codes and PAYE tax tables, effective from 11 May 1983, based on the bands proposed in the 1983 Budget Resolutions. Although FA 1983 retained the 1982–83 tax bands, s 10 (3) of that Act provided for the revised codes and tables to be applied by employers until 31 August 1983. As a result of the enactment of F(No 2)A 1983 s 1, these codes and tables will remain valid after that date.

2 Corporation tax: small companies

(1) In section 13 of the Finance Act 1983, for the words "seventy-fifths" there shall be substituted the words "two-hundredths".

(2) For the financial year 1982 and subsequent financial years subsection (3) of section 95 of the Finance Act 1972 (marginal relief for small companies) shall have effect with the substitution for any reference to £90,000 of a reference to £100,000 and with the substitution for any reference to £225,000 of a reference to £500,000.

(3) Where, by virtue of subsection (2) above, the said section 95 has effect with different relevant amounts in relation to different parts of the same accounting period, those parts shall be treated for the purposes of that section as if they were separate accounting periods and the profits and income of the company for that period (as defined in that section) shall be apportioned between those parts.

SMALL COMPANIES RATE

By FA 1983 s 13 the reduced rate of corporation tax on the income of companies whose profits do not exceed the lower profits limit was fixed at 38 per cent for the financial year 1982.

PROFITS LIMITS (SUB-S (2))

The lower and upper profits limits are increased to £100,000 and £500,000 respectively with effect for the financial year 1982 and subsequent years.

MARGINAL RELIEF (SUB-S (1))

Where a company's profits fall between the lower and upper limits, the income is charged to the full rate of corporation tax subject to marginal relief. The accelerating fraction to be used in the calculation of the marginal relief for the financial year 1982 and subsequent years to take account of the increased profits limits is 7/200ths. The effective rate of tax on the profits falling between these limits is therefore 55½ per cent.

ACCOUNTING PERIODS STRADDLING FINANCIAL YEARS (SUB-S (3))

Where different profits limits apply to different parts of the same accounting period (as, for instance, where an accounting period begins before and ends after 1 April 1982) those parts are treated as if they were separate accounting periods and the profits and income of the company for the complete period are apportioned between them for the purposes of determining the appropriate rates of corporation tax.

EXAMPLE

A Ltd has profits of £210,000 (all income for the year ended 30 November 1982.

	Proportion of profit	*Proportion of upper limit*	*Proportion of lower limit*
	£	£	£
1.12.81–31.3.82	70,000	75,000	30,000
1.4.82–30.11.82	140,000	333,333	66,667

For each part of the period the profits exceed the appropriate proportion of the lower limit and the marginal relief provisions apply. The corporation tax payable is as follows—

1.12.81–31.3.82:	£70,000 @ 52%	£36,400	
	Deduct: 2/25 × (£75,000–70,000)	400	
			£36,000
1.4.82–30.11.82:	£140,000 @ 52%	£72,800	
	Deduct: 7/200 × (333,333–140,000)	6,767	
			£66,033
Corporation tax payable for accounting period ended 30.11.82			£102,033

3 Relief for interest

(1) For the year 1983–84, the limit referred to in sub-paragraph (1) of paragraph 5 of Schedule 1 to the Finance Act 1974 (limit on relief for interest on certain loans for the purchase or improvement of land) shall be £30,000, subject to any reduction falling to be made under that paragraph; and accordingly, for that year, for any reference in that sub-paragraph to £25,000 there shall be substituted a reference to £30,000.

(2) For the year 1983–84, in paragraph 24 (3) of that Schedule (loans to purchase life annuities) for any reference to £25,000 there shall be substituted a reference to £30,000.

GENERAL NOTE

For 1983–84, tax relief will be given for the interest paid on loans up to £30,000 for the purchase or improvement of the borrower's only or main residence (or that of a dependent relative or of a former or separated spouse). The limit was formerly £25,000. For that year, the limit on loans eligible for relief when used by a person over 65 for the purchase of a life annuity and secured on his main residence is also increased from £25,000 to £30,000.

PAYE

The £25,000 limit was not increased by FA 1983. However, Resolution 15 of the March 1983 Budget Resolutions had provided for the limit to be increased to £30,000. As a consequence, before the enactment of FA 1983, revised PAYE codings were issued to those taxpayers with mortgages over £25,000 who did not come within the system of mortgage interest relief at source (MIRAS) or who paid tax at the higher rates. FA 1983 s 16 (2), (3) enabled employers to continue using those codes when calculating PAYE deductions until 31 August 1983. As a result of the enactment of F(No 2)A 1983 s 3, these codes will remain valid after that date.

4 Loans obtained by reason of employment

At the end of Part III of Schedule 8 to the Finance Act 1976 (taxation of benefit from loans obtained by reason of employment: exceptions where interest eligible for relief) there shall be added the following paragraphs—

"**12**—(1) If, in the year 1983–84 or any subsequent year of assessment,—

(*a*) a person has a loan on which no interest is paid and of which the benefit was obtained by reason of his or any other person's employment (in this paragraph referred to as "the employer's loan"), and

(*b*) that person or his wife or husband has another loan which was made later than, or at the same time as, the employer's loan and interest on which is, in whole or in part, eligible for relief,

then, for the purposes of determining whether, had interest been paid on the employer's loan at the official rate, the whole or any part of that interest would have been eligible for relief, Schedule 1 to the Finance Act 1974 shall have effect as if the employer's loan were made after any other loan which falls within paragraph (*b*) above and which, in the context of the application of Part I of Schedule 9 to the Finance Act 1972, relates to the same land, caravan or house boat as does the employer's loan.

(2) Where such a loan is made as is mentioned in paragraph (*b*) of sub-paragraph (1) above, Schedule 1 to the Finance Act 1974 has effect in accordance with that sub-paragraph with respect to so much of the interest referred to therein as would be paid on and after the day on which the loan is made; and paragraph 11 (3) above shall have effect for the purpose of determining how much of that interest would have been eligible for relief.

13—(1) Where in any year a person has, alone or together with his wife or husband, two or more loans—

(*a*) on which no interest is paid, and

(*b*) which, assuming the application of Part I of Schedule 9 to the Finance Act 1972, would relate, in the context of that Part, to the same land, caravan or house boat,

then, for the purpose of determining whether, had interest been paid on any of those loans, it would, in whole or in part, have been eligible for relief, it shall be assumed in the first instance that those loans constitute a single loan (equal in amount to the aggregate of the actual loans) and to the extent that, had interest been paid on that single loan, it would have been eligible for relief, the relief shall then be attributed first to the earliest of the actual loans and, if all the relief is not thereby attributed, the balance shall be attributed to the next in time and so on with any of the balance remaining until the relief is wholly attributed.

(2) Nothing in sub-paragraph (1) above affects the operation of paragraph 12 above in relation to the priority which it gives to a loan falling within sub-paragraph (1) (*b*) of that paragraph, but any question which of two or more loans falling within sub-paragraph (1) above is the earlier shall be determined without regard to that paragraph.

14 References in paragraphs 12 and 13 above to a husband or wife do not include references to a separated husband or wife."

GENERAL NOTE

Relief is available for interest on loans incurred for the purchase or improvement of land, a caravan, or a houseboat for use as the only or main residence of the borrower, a dependent relative of his, or his former or separated spouse (FA 1974 Sch 1 paras 4(1)(*a*), 4A(1)). The relief for interest on the aggregate of such loans is restricted. The interest is eligible for relief only to the extent that the amounts on which interest is payable by the borrower on such loans in the year of assessment do not exceed a maximum limit (FA 1974 Sch 1 para 5(1); the limit is £30,000 for 1983–84).

A loan on which no interest whatsoever is payable is not therefore taken into account in applying that limit.

If an interest-free loan is made to a person by reason of his employment (or the employment of a relative of his as defined in FA 1976 s 66 (10)), the benefit of the loan may be taxable on the employee as an emolument of the employment (FA 1976 s 66 (1)). The benefit of the loan is determined by calculating interest thereon at an official rate (12 per cent from 6 October 1982), see FA 1976 Sch 8 para 5(2)(*a*). But insofar as any such interest would, if if had actually been payable, have been eligible for relief, it is excluded from the calculation of the benefit.

If the interest-free loan was made before any loan on which interest was payable, the relief limit in 1982–83 and earlier years was available to the full extent to reduce or eliminate the benefit taxable on the employee and yet, in determining the eligibility of the subsequent interest-bearing loan the relief limit was again available to the full extent because the earlier loan, being free of interest, did not have to be taken into account. In this way a borrower could effectively double the total amount of loans on which he could obtain relief.

The paragraphs added to FA 1976 Sch 8 by this section are intended to stop this for 1983–84 and later years.

ORDER OF LOANS FOR INTEREST RELIEF (FA 1976 SCH 8 PARA 12)

In 1983–84 and any later year of assessment, if a person has an interest-free loan made by reason of his (or his relative's) employment as well as a loan on which interest is payable and which is wholly or partly eligible for relief, the £30,000 limit is applied to the loans as if the interest-free loan was made after the other one.

Accordingly the amount excluded from the benefit taxable on the employee in respect of the employer's loan is restricted by reference to the balance, if any, of the relief available to the borrower.

This does not apply unless the loans relate to the same land, caravan, or houseboat.

Where an interest-bearing loan is made during the course of the year of assessment, any consequential reduction in the amount excluded from the benefit taxable on the employee in respect of the employer's loan enters into the calculation of the benefit only for the period after the date on which the new loan was made (FA 1976 Sch 8 para 12 (2)). The official rate must be calculated for this purpose on a daily basis on the maximum amount outstanding under the employee's loan on each day (FA 1976 Sch 8 para 11).

EXAMPLE 1

E has a loan of £25,000 interest-free from his employer. It was made on 31 March 1983 and applied by E in the purchase of the house in which he resides.

On 6 July 1983 E borrows £10,000 from a building society to finance improvements to the house.

The interest on the building society loan is eligible for relief in full.

The taxable benefit in respect of the interest-free loan for the period from 6 April 1983 to 5 July 1983 is nil because the amount of the loan is less than the relief limit for 1983–84—£30,000—and there are no other loans eligible for relief. The taxable benefit for the rest of the year (assuming an official rate of 12 per cent throughout) is £450: calculated in accordance with FA 1976 Sch 8 para 6—

$$\pounds(25{,}000 + 25{,}000) \div 2 \times \frac{5{,}000}{25{,}000} \times \tfrac{9}{12} \times 12\% = \pounds 450$$

The result of the alternative calculation under para 7 is virtually the same because the amount of the employer's loan does not fluctuate during the period.

MORE THAN ONE INTEREST-FREE LOAN (FA 1976 SCH 8 PARA 13)

An interest-free loan which is not an employer's loan can affect the extent to which relief is available to reduce the taxable benefit on an employer's loan made subsequently. If a person has more than one interest-free loan in relation to the same property, the notional relief which would have been allowable if interest had been payable on those loans is restricted by reference to the £30,000 limit as follows: the notional relief on the aggregate of those loans (including those which are not employer's loans) is attributed to the individual loans in the order in which they were made.

If an employer's loan which is interest-free is made before some other interest-free loan but after a loan under which interest is payable which is wholly or partly eligible for relief, the effect of para 12 (1) is that the employer's loan is treated as made after the interest-bearing loan. This is, however, ignored in determining the order in which the interest-free loans were made.

EXAMPLE 2

In 1982 D borrowed £28,000 to purchase a house as his only residence. The borrowing comprised two loans—

(1) £25,000 at interest from a building society:
(2) £3,000 interest-free from D's aunt.

Both loans remain outstanding throughout 1983–84.

On 6 October 1983 D's employer lends him £5,000 interest-free to pay for improvements to the house.

In 1983–84 the building society loan interest is eligible for relief in full. There is no income tax liability or relief for D in respect of the loan from his aunt. His aunt's loan is taken into account however in determining the amount of the benefit taxable on D in respect of the loan from his employer.

	£
Loan from aunt	3,000
Employer's loan	5,000
Total interest-free	8,000
Relief limit	30,000
Building society loan	25,000
Amount on which interest would have been eligible for relief	5,000

The notional relief is attributed as to £3,000 to the loan from D's aunt and only the balance of £2,000 is available to reduce the taxable benefit in respect of the employer's loan.

Accordingly the benefit assessable on D for 1983–84 would be (applying FA 1976 Sch 8 para 6)—

$$£5{,}000 \times \frac{3{,}000}{5{,}000} \times \frac{6}{12} \times 12\% = £180$$

HUSBAND AND WIFE

Unless the taxpayer and his spouse are separated (FA 1976 Sch 8 para 14), interest-bearing loans made to his spouse in the year of assessment are to be taken into account for the purposes of these provisions if they relate to the same property as the employer's loan (para 12(1)(*b*)). Similarly any other interest-free loans relating to that property but made to the taxpayer's spouse are to be taken into account in determining the availability of the notional relief to reduce the benefit taxable in respect of the employer's loan (para 13 (1)).

Spouses are "separated" where they are living apart pursuant to a court order or deed of separation or otherwise in circumstances in which their separation is likely to be permanent (TA 1970 s 42 (1) and compare FA 1974 Sch 1 para 4(4)(*b*)).

5 Relief for investment in corporate trades

(1) Schedule 1 to this Act shall have effect for the purpose of making miscellaneous amendments of Part I of Schedule 5 to the Finance Act 1983 (relief for investment in corporate trades).

(2) The amendments made by Schedule 1 to this Act shall be deemed to have been incorporated in Part I of Schedule 5 as originally enacted.

GENERAL NOTE

The business expansion scheme was introduced by FA 1983 to replace the business start up scheme, for investments after 5 April 1983. The curtailment of debate brought about by the announcement of the general election resulted in the original provisions being enacted unamended, as FA 1983 s 26 and Sch 5.

This section introduces Schedule 1, which contains technical amendments to the FA 1983 Sch 5 provisions. No changes are made to the basic features of the scheme.

6 Allowances for dwelling-houses let on assured tenancies

(1) In Schedule 12 to the Finance Act 1982 (capital allowances for dwelling-houses let on assured tenancies) in paragraph 4 (5) (*c*) for the words from "there were" to "both" there shall be substituted the words "and the word 'if' preceding them there were substituted the words 'unless both' ".

(2) The amendment made by subsection (1) above shall be deemed always to have had effect, except that it shall not affect the validity of any election under paragraph 4 of Schedule 7 to the Capital Allowances Act 1968 which was made before 1st April 1983 in reliance on the provisions of paragraph 4(5)(*c*) of Schedule 12 to the Finance Act 1982, as originally enacted.

(3) In subsection (4) of section 34 of the Capital Gains Tax Act 1979 (definition of "capital allowance") at the end of paragraph (*a*) there shall be inserted the following paragraph—

"(*aa*) an allowance under Schedule 12 to the Finance Act 1982".

(4) The amendment made by subsection (3) above shall be deemed always to have had effect, except that it shall not affect the computation under Chapter II of Part II of the Capital Gains Tax Act 1979 of the amount of any loss accruing on a disposal before 1st April 1983.

(5) In paragraph 3 of Schedule 12 to the Finance Act 1982 (definition of "qualifying dwelling-house") in subparagraph (3)(*a*) after the words "unless the landlord" there shall be inserted the words "is a company and either".

(6) The amendment made by subsection (5) above shall have effect in relation to—

(*a*) expenditure incurred on or after 5th May 1983 otherwise than pursuant to a contract entered into before that date by the person incurring the expenditure, and

(*b*) expenditure which, by virtue of paragraph 8 of Schedule 12 to the Finance Act 1982, is deemed to be incurred on or after that date,

and also in any case where a person other than a company becomes entitled to the relevant interest, within the meaning of that Schedule, on or after that date.

GENERAL NOTE

This section corrects two drafting errors in the provisions (FA 1982 s 76, Sch 12) relating to capital allowances for buildings let on assured tenancies granted pursuant to the Housing Act 1980. A further amendment is made to ensure that such allowances are available only to companies.

SALES WITHOUT CHANGE OF CONTROL (SUB-SS (1), (2))

Where capital allowances have been given in respect of a building and the building is subsequently sold, there are special provisions to deal with the situation in which the vendor and purchaser are under common control or one of them controls the other (CAA 1968 Sch 7). These provisions were applied to buildings let on assured tenancies by FA 1982 Sch 12 Para 4 (5). The correction of para 4(5)(*e*) ensures that on the sale in such circumstances of a building let on an assured tenancy, the parties may elect for the purchaser to take over the vendor's residue of expenditure with no balancing charge being made on the vendor if, and only if, both vendor and purchaser are approved bodies for the purposes of the assured tenancies scheme. The original wording inadvertently had the effect of excluding the right of election in just the case where both parties were approved bodies.

This amendment is deemed always to have had effect. However, an election made before 1 April 1983 where the purchaser was not an approved body and the parties relied on the original wording, is not invalidated by the amendment.

RESTRICTION OF LOSSES (SUB-SS (3), (4))

Losses allowable for CGT are restricted by excluding from the deductible expenditure any amounts in respect of which certain specified capital allowances have been made. Those capital allowances are set out in CGTA 1979 s 34 (4). When capital allowances for buildings let on assured tenancies were introduced, these allowances were not added to those referred to in the restriction. This omission is now made good. Accordingly, save as regards losses accruing on a disposal before 1 April 1983, any expenditure on such a building for which capital allowances have been or may be made is not deductible in computing the allowable loss, if any, on the disposal of the building.

QUALIFYING DWELLINGHOUSE (SUB-SS (5), (6))

To qualify for capital allowances under FA 1982 Sch 12, the expenditure must be incurred on the construction of a building as, or including, a dwellinghouse for letting on an assured tenancy under the Housing Act 1980 s 56.

One of the conditions for the creation of an assured tenancy is that the landlord must be a body approved by the Secretary of State under the Housing Act 1980 s 56 (4). Generally applicants for such approval have been bodies corporate, but at least one partnership has been approved and approval is not refused merely because the applicant is an unincorporated body of persons (see HC Debates (12 July 1983) Vol 45 col 845).

It is intended that capital allowances for expenditure on buildings let on assured tenancies should only be available to companies. Accordingly the conditions to be satisfied in relation to a building if it is to be a qualifying dwellinghouse are amended to include the requirement that the landlord (who must either have incurred the expenditure or be the body entitled for the time being to the relevant interest in the building—FA 1982 Sch 12 para 3(3)(*a*)) must be a company.

Generally this amendment takes effect on 5 May 1983. Hence it applies to expenditure incurred after 4 May 1983 and where the relevant interest in the building is transferred after that date to an unincorporated body. If the building is sold unused, the expenditure which is deemed to be incurred by the purchaser when the purchase price becomes payable (FA 1982 Sch 12 para 8(1)(*b*)) does not qualify for capital allowances if the purchaser is not a company and the purchase price becomes payable after 4 May 1983.

However, if expenditure on the construction of the building is incurred by a contracting party pursuant to a contract entered into before 5 May 1983, the amendment does not apply to that party.

7 Relief for local constituency associations of political parties on reorganisation of constituencies

(1) In this section "relevant date" means the date of coming into operation of an Order in Council under section 3 of the House of Commons (Redistribution of Seats) Act 1949 (orders specifying new parliamentary constituencies) and, in relation to any relevant date,—

(*a*) "former parliamentary constituency" means an area which, for the purposes of parliamentary elections, was a constituency immediately before that date but is no longer such a constituency after that date; and

(*b*) "new parliamentary constituency" means an area which, for the purposes of parliamentary elections, is a constituency immediately after that date but was not such a constituency before that date.

(2) In this section "local constituency association" means an unincorporated association (whether described as an association, a branch or otherwise) whose primary purpose is to further the aims of a political party in an area which at any time is or was the same or substantially the same as the area of a parliamentary constituency or two or more parliamentary constituencies and, in relation to any relevant date,—

(*a*) "existing association" means a local constituency association whose area was the same, or substantially the same, as the area of a former parliamentary constituency or two or more such constituencies; and

(*b*) "new association" means a local constituency association whose area is the same, or substantially the same, as the area of a new parliamentary constituency or two or more such constituencies.

(3) For the purposes of this section, a new association is a successor to an existing association if any part of the existing association's area is comprised in the new association's area,

(4) In any case where, before, on or after a relevant date,—

(*a*) an existing association disposes of land to a new association which is a successor to the existing association, or

(*b*) an existing association disposes of land to a body (whether corporate or unincorporated) which is an organ of the political party concerned and, as soon as practicable thereafter, that body disposes of the land to a new association which is a successor to the existing association,

the parties to the disposal or, where paragraph (*b*) above applies, to each of the disposals, shall be treated for the purposes of corporation tax in respect of chargeable gains or, as the case may require, capital gains tax as if the land disposed of were acquired from the existing association or the body making the disposal for a consideration of such an amount as would secure that on the disposal neither a gain nor a loss accrued to that association or body.

(5) In a case falling within subsection (4) above, the new association shall be treated for the purposes of Schedule 5 to the Capital Gains Tax Act 1979 (assets held on 6th April 1965) as if the acquisition by the existing association of the land disposed of as mentioned in that subsection had been the new association's acquisition of it; and in paragraph 3 of Schedule 13 to the Finance Act 1982 (indexation: subsequent disposals following a no gain/no loss disposal) at the end of sub-paragraph (3) there shall be added—

"(*d*) subsection (4) of section 7 of the Finance (No 2) Act 1983".

(6) In any case where—

(*a*) before, on or after a relevant date, an existing association disposes of any land which was used and occupied by it for the purposes of its functions, and

(*b*) the existing association transfers the whole or part of the proceeds of the disposal to a new association which is a successor to the existing association,

then, subject to subsection (7) below, the Capital Gains Tax Act 1979 (and, in particular, the provisions of sections 115 to 121 providing for roll-over relief on the replacement of business assets) shall have effect as if, since the time it was acquired by the existing association, the land disposed of had been the property of the new association and, accordingly, as if the disposal of it had been by the new association.

(7) If, in a case falling within subsection (6) above, only part of the proceeds of the disposal is transferred to the new association, that subsection shall apply—

(*a*) as if there existed in the land disposed of as mentioned in paragraph (*a*) of that subsection a separate asset in the form of a corresponding undivided share in that land, and subject to any necessary apportionments of consideration for an acquisition or disposal of, or of an interest in, that land; and

(*b*) as if the references in that subsection (other than paragraph (*a*) thereof) to the land disposed of and the disposal of it were references respectively to the corresponding undivided share referred to in paragraph (*a*) above and the disposal of that share;

and for this purpose a corresponding undivided share in the land disposed of is a share which bears to the whole of that land the same proportion as the part of the proceeds transferred bears to the whole of those proceeds.

(8) In this section "political party" means a political party which qualifies for exemption under paragraph 11 of Schedule 6 to the Finance Act 1975 (gifts to political parties).

(9) This section applies in any case where the relevant date falls after 1st January 1983 and the disposal referred to in subsection (4) or subsection (6) above is on or after 6th April 1983.

GENERAL NOTE

This section is designed to exempt from a capital gains charge the transfer of land by political party constituency associations as a result of the reorganisation of constituency boundaries prior to the 1983 general election. It provides that such transfers and all future transfers following future reorganisations shall be on a no gain/no loss basis.

DEFINITIONS

A "local constituency association" means an unincorporated body, however described, whose primary purpose is to further the aims of a political party in an area substantially the same as the area of one or more parliamentary constituencies. An "existing" association is one organised around the boundaries of one or more former constituencies (a parliamentary constituency that ceases to be one after the relevant date—see below); a "new" association is one organised around the boundaries of one or more new constituencies (a parliamentary constituency that comes into being on the relevant date).

A new association is a successor to an existing association if *any part* of the existing association's area falls into the new association's area.

The meaning of political party is limited to a party qualifying for exemption under the capital transfer tax provisions (FA 1975 Sch 6 para 11) for gifts to political parties. In order to qualify, a party must have had at least two members elected to the House of Commons *at the last general election* or one member elected and at least 150,000 votes cast for its candidates. It is not clear whether this should be the election immediately preceding the relevant date or preceding the transfer of the property. On the votes cast at the general election on 9 June 1983 the following parties would qualify—

(*a*) the Conservative Party;
(*b*) the Labour Party;
(*c*) the Liberal Party;
(*d*) the Official Unionist Party;
(*e*) the Social Democratic Party;
(*f*) the Democratic Unionist Party;
(*g*) the Scottish National Party;
(*h*) Plaid Cymru.

A relevant date is the date of the coming into force of an Order in Council under the House of Commons (Redistribution of Seats) Act 1949 s 3. The four existing such orders are—

(*a*) the Parliamentary Constituencies (Northern Ireland) Order, SI 1982/1838; coming into operation 5.1.83;
(*b*) the Parliamentary Constituencies (Wales) Order, SI 1983/418; coming into operation 30.3.83;
(*c*) the Parliamentary Constituencies (Scotland) Order, SI 1983/422; coming into operation 30.3.83;
(*d*) the Parliamentary Constituencies (England) Order, SI 1983/417; coming into operation 30.3.83.

QUALIFYING DISPOSALS

Where—

(*a*) an existing association disposes of land directly to a successor new association *or*
(*b*) an existing association disposes of land to an organ (which can be a corporate or an unincorporated body) of the particular political party and that organ then disposes, as soon as practicable, of that land to a successor new association

the disposal or disposals is/are treated as made on a no gain/no loss basis to the disponer. The disposal may take place at any time before or after the relevant date.

ASSETS HELD ON 6 APRIL 1965

When such a disposal or disposals is/are made, the new association is deemed for the purposes of CGTA 1979 Sch 5 (assets held on 6 April 1965) to have acquired the land when it was acquired by the existing association, even where the disposal takes place through the intermediary body.

INDEXATION

When a disposal is made between associations on a no gain/no loss basis as above, the continuity of the indexation allowance, provided by FA 1982 Sch 13 para 3, is maintained. Such disposals will be accorded the same treatment as eg, transfers between husband and wife.

ROLLOVER RELIEF

If the existing association disposes of any land occupied or used by it for the purposes of its functions and transfers all or part of the proceeds to a succcessor new association, the new association is deemed for the purposes of CGTA 1979 to have been the owner of the land since it was acquired by the existing association and to have disposed of it itself. This applies in particular to rollover relief on the replacement of business assets (CGTA 1979 ss 115–121). Rollover relief is extended (CGTA 1979 s 21(1) (*e*)) to unincorporated associations chargeable to corporation tax whose activities are carried on wholly or mainly otherwise than for profit and the Revenue has confirmed that it extends also to assets owned by a company which is in turn owned by an unincorporated association.

If only part of the proceeds of disposal are transferred by the existing association to the new association, the above provisions apply as if a separate asset in the form of an undivided share of the land had been disposed of. The undivided share of the land is in the same proportion to the whole of the land disposed of by the existing association as the part of the proceeds transferred bears to the entire proceeds.

DATE OF APPLICATION

The relevant date must fall after 1 January 1983 and the disposal must take place after 5 April 1983. Consequently, disposals by associations that took place before 6 April 1983 are not retrospectively exempted.

DISPOSALS BY COMPANIES

Since a local constituency association is expressly defined as being an *unincorporated* association, the provisions do not apply to disposals by companies holding land on behalf of constituency associations. The Financial Secretary to the Treasury has said (HC Official Report 12 July 1983 Vol 45 cols 846–7) that the Government is prepared to examine sympathetically the case for extending the provisions if this should cause problems in practice.

PART II
CAPITAL TRANSFER TAX

8 Reduction of tax

(1) Section 91 (1) of the Finance Act 1982 (indexation of rate bands) shall not apply to chargeable transfers made in the year beginning with 6th April 1983.

(2) For the Tables in section 37 (3) of the Finance Act 1975 there shall be substituted the Tables set out below.

FIRST TABLE

Portion of value		Rate of tax
Lower limit	Upper limit	Per cent
£	£	
0	60,000	Nil
60,000	80,000	30
80,000	110,000	35
110,000	140,000	40
140,000	175,000	45
175,000	220,000	50
220,000	270,000	55
270,000	700,000	60
700,000	1,325,000	65
1,325,000	2,650,000	70
2,650,000	—	75

SECOND TABLE

Portion of value		Rate of tax
Lower limit	Upper limit	Per cent
£	£	
0	60,000	Nil
60,000	80,000	15
80,000	110,000	$17\frac{1}{2}$
110,000	140,000	20
140,000	175,000	$22\frac{1}{2}$
175,000	220,000	25
220,000	270,000	30
270,000	700,000	35
700,000	1,325,000	40
1,325,000	2,650,000	45
2,650,000	—	50

(3) Subsection (2) above applies to any chargeable transfer made on or after 15th March 1983.

GENERAL NOTE

FA 1982 s 91 introduced indexation of the CTT rate bands from 6 April in each year by reference to the increase in the index of retail prices in the previous calendar year, unless Parliament otherwise determines.

It has been decided this year to determine otherwise in the form of new rate bands which represent a rounding up of the rate bands, beyond the level which the indexation rules would produce, to multiples of £5,000 or £10,000 (and not always to the nearest such multiple). Also, these new bands apply to any chargeable transfer made on or after 15 March 1983.

The indexation provisions of FA 1982 s 91 will continue to be capable of applying in future years, and if they are not overridden by specific legislation next year they will operate to increase the rate bands set out in this section in proportion to the increase in the index of retail prices between December 1982 and December 1983.

9 Gifts to charities

(1) In paragraph 10 (1) of Schedule 6 to the Finance Act 1975 (exemption from tax for gifts to charities), paragraph (*b*) (which limits the exemption to £250,000 in respect of gifts on or within one year of the death of the transferor) shall cease to have effect.

(2) In section 117 of the Finance Act 1976 (modification of exemptions for loans) in subsection (5)—

(*a*) for the words "Paragraphs 10 and 11 (gifts to charities and" there shall be substituted the words "Paragraph 11 (gifts"; and

(*b*) for the words from "those paragraphs" to "13 (gifts" there shall be substituted the words "that paragraph and paragraphs 10, 12 and 13 (gifts to charities,".

(3) This section has effect in relation to transfers of value made on or after 15th March 1983.

GENERAL NOTE

This removes in relation to transfers made on or after 15 March 1983 the limit on the amount or value of property which may be transferred to charity on or within one year of the death of the transferor in such manner as to qualify for exemption from CTT. Subsection (2) is a consequential amendment.

10 Relief for business and agricultural property

(1) The appropriate percentage in the case of property falling within paragraph 3 (1) (*bb*) of Schedule 10 to the Finance Act 1976 (relief for minority shareholdings in unquoted companies) shall be increased from 20 per cent to 30 per cent and accordingly in paragraph 2 (1A) of that Schedule—

(*a*) paragraph (*b*) shall cease to have effect; and

(*b*) in paragraph (*c*), after the words "3 (1)" there shall be inserted the words "(*bb*),".

(2) In sub-paragraphs (2) and (4) of paragraph 2 of Schedule 14 to the Finance Act 1981 (appropriate percentage in relation to relief for agricultural property) for the words "20 per cent" there shall, in each case, be substituted the words "30 per cent".

(3) This section has effect in relation to transfers of value made, and other events occurring, on or after 15th March 1983.

GENERAL NOTE

FA 1976 Sch 10 para 3(1)(*bb*) provides for a reduction of 20 per cent in the value of any holding of unquoted shares included in a transfer of value and which qualifies for business relief but is not entitled to the 50 per cent rate of relief because it does not carry sufficient votes to control the company.

For transfers made after 14 March 1983 the rate of business relief for such holdings of shares is increased to 30 per cent.

With the elimination of the 20 per cent rate there are now only two rates of business relief—50 per cent and 30 per cent.

FA 1981 Sch 14 para 2(2) and (4) provides for a reduction of 20 per cent in the value of any agricultural property included in a transfer of value and which qualifies for agricultural relief but is not entitled to the 50 per cent rate of relief because, for example, the transferor did not have vacant possession of the property immediately before the transfer or the right to obtain it within the following 12 months.

For transfers made after 14 March 1983 the 20 per cent rate of agricultural relief is increased to 30 per cent.

11 Payment of tax by instalments

(1) In paragraphs 13 (1), 14 (1) and 15 of Schedule 4 to the Finance Act 1975 (cases in which tax may be paid by instalments) for the words "at his option either by eight equal yearly instalments or by sixteen equal half-yearly instalments" there shall be substituted the words "by ten equal yearly instalments".

(2) In paragraph 13 (3) of Schedule 4 (conditions applying in relation to transfers of certain shares) for the words "£5,000" there shall be substituted the words "£20,000".

(3) This section has effect in relation to chargeable transfers made on or after 15th March 1983.

GENERAL NOTE

At present there is (under FA 1975 Sch 4 paras 13–15) an option to pay CTT by instalments of either (at the option of the taxpayer) 8 yearly or 16 half-yearly instalments when the CTT is attributable to business property, controlling shareholdings, certain minority unquoted shareholdings, land, or timber, if certain conditions are fulfilled.

Subsection (1) increases the period over which the instalments may be paid to ten years but abolishes the right to pay in half-yearly instalments, in relation to chargeable transfers made on or after 15 March 1983.

Subsection (2) increases from £5,000 to £20,000 the minimum value a minority unquoted holding must have to qualify for the instalment option under FA 1975 Sch 4 para 13(1)(*d*) as from the same date.

12 Domicile

(1) Section 45 (1) (*c*) of the Finance Act 1975 (which treats certain persons who have become domiciled in the Channel Islands or in the Isle of Man as domiciled in the United Kingdom) shall cease to have effect.

(2) This section has effect in relation to transfers of value made, and other events occurring, on or after 15th March 1983.

GENERAL NOTE

This abolishes the rule that someone who changed his domicile from the UK to the Channel Islands or Isle of Man after 10 December 1974 is treated as retaining a UK domicile for CTT purposes.

The abolition has effect for transfers of value made and events occurring on or after 15 March 1983, but in relation to transferors who changed to an Islands' domicile before that date (as well as ones who change domicile after it). It is not entirely clear whether a settlement made between 10 December 1974 and 15 March 1983 by a settlor who was at the time of making the settlement treated as UK domiciled by reason only of FA 1975 s 45(1)(*c*) will in relation to occasions of CTT charge on or after 15 March 1983 be treated as made by a non-UK domiciled settlor.

13 Burden of tax

(1) In section 28 of the Finance Act 1975 (burden of tax) the following subsections shall be substituted for subsection (1)—

"(1) Where personal representatives are liable for tax on the value transferred by a chargeable transfer made on death, the tax shall be treated as part of the general testamentary and administration expenses of the estate, but only so far as it is attributable to the value of property in the United Kingdom which—

(*a*) vests in the deceased's personal representatives; and

(*b*) was not, immediately before the death, comprised in a settlement.

The provision made by this subsection shall have effect subject to any contrary intention shown by the deceased in his will.

(1A) Where any amount of tax paid by personal representatives on the value transferred by a chargeable transfer made on death does not fall to be borne as part of the general testamentary and administration expenses of the estate, that amount shall, where occasion requires, be repaid to them by the person in whom the property to the value of which the tax is attributable is vested."

(2) For subsection (8) of that section there shall be substituted—

"(8) References in this section (except subsection (2)) to tax include references to interest on tax and, in subsections (3) to (5), to costs properly incurred in respect of tax."

(3) This section has effect where the death or other event on which tax is chargeable occurs on or after the day on which this Act is passed.

GENERAL NOTE

FA 1975 s 28 and Sch 4 para 20 were intended to preserve the estate duty rules as to incidence in relation to CTT. One of the estate duty rules was that in the absence of a contrary declaration, freehold land comprised in a deceased persons' estate would bear its own duty (while the duty on personalty situated in the UK was a testamentary expense payable out of residue in the absence of directions to the contrary). However, it was held in *Re Dougal* [1981] STC 514 that in Scotland CTT on realty is a testamentary expense and payable out of residue (in the absence of a contrary direction) in the same way as the CTT on personalty. It is thought by many, including the Revenue, that the reasons relied on by the court in *Re Dougal* would apply equally in England, but the pount is not free from doubt.

Section 13 resolves the uncertainties of the law as it stands at the moment, in favour of the rule laid down in *Re Dougal,* but only in relation to the estates of persons who die on or after 26 July 1983 (the day on which the Act was passed). It will apply to the estates of persons who die on or after that date even though they leave wills made before it, which may have been made on the (unexpressed) assumption that realty bears its own estate duty or CTT.

Section 13 also makes it clear that property situated outside the UK and comprised in an estate will continue to bear its own duty.

Subsection (2) alters FA 1975 s 28(8) in two ways: first, s 28(8) no longer applies to FA 1975 s 28(2), but its formerly doing so was inappropriate or redundant, and so this makes no practical difference, and secondly references to tax in what, when this section takes effect, will be FA 1975 s 28(1A) (formerly s 28(1)) will no longer include costs properly incurred in respect of tax, so that personal representatives will no longer have a right to reinbursement of such costs where they pay tax for which some other person is ultimately liable.

Part III
Miscellaneous and Supplementary

14 Development land tax: certain operations relating to telecommunications not to be development

(1) In section 47 of the Development Land Tax Act 1976 (interpretation) in subsection (1), in the definition of "development" and "development order" after the word "have" there shall be inserted the words "subject to subsections (1A) and (1B) below".

(2) After the said subsection (1) there shall be inserted the following subsections—

"(1A) In this Act the expression "development" does not include operations which are begun on or before 31st December 1984 and are carried out for the purposes of—

(*a*) the laying of telecommunications cables;

(*b*) the installation of troughs to house telecommunications cables;

(*c*) the erection or construction of structures to house signal regeneration equipment or the installation of such equipment.

(1B) In subsection (1A) above the expressions "trough" and "structure"—

(*a*) do not include any trough or structure the height of which above ground level exceeds three metres; and

(*b*) except in the case of a trough to house telecommunications cables, do not include any structure which covers an area of ground in excess of five square metres."

GENERAL NOTE

A charge to development land tax arises on the commencement of a project of material development.

For the purposes of development land tax, "development" is defined as the carrying out of building, engineering, mining or other operations in, on, over or under land, or the making of any material change in use of any buildings or other land (the Town and Country Planning Act 1971 ss 22, 290, applied by DLTA 1976 s 47).

But for the amendments made to DLTA 1976 s 47 by this section, many of the operations carried out by companies which set up telecommunications networks under the provisions of the Telecommunications Bill 1983 would be projects of material development giving rise to a charge to development land tax.

DLTA 1976 s 47 (1A), (1B), inserted by this section, exclude cable laying and certain closely related operations from the definition of "development" and so prevent a charge to development land tax arising. The exemption does not extend to the construction of substantial structures such as administration and control buildings.

The relief provided under this section is restricted to operations begun before 1 January 1985. It is proposed that operations begun on or after that date will be exempted under a revised general development order. (The present order, the Town and Country Planning General Development Order, SI 1977/289, only covers activities undertaken by British Telecom.)

15 Relief from stamp duty for local constituency associations of political parties on reorganisation of constituencies

(1) In a case falling within paragraph (*a*) or paragraph (*b*) of subsection (4) of section 7 above—

(*a*) no stamp duty shall be chargeable under section **74** of the Finance (1909–10) Act 1910 (gifts inter vivos) on a conveyance or transfer by which the disposal or, in the case of paragraph (*b*), either of the disposals referred to in that paragraph is effected; and

(*b*) section **57** of the Stamp Act 1891 shall not apply in relation to such a conveyance or transfer as is referred to in paragraph (*a*) above.

(2) An instrument in respect of which stamp duty under the said section **74** is not chargeable by virtue only of subsection (1) above shall not be treated as duly stamped unless—

(*a*) it has, in accordance with the provisions of section 12 of the Stamp Act 1891, been stamped with a particular stamp denoting either that it is duly stamped or that it is not chargeable with any duty; or

(*b*) it is stamped with the duty to which it would but for subsection (1) above be liable.

GENERAL NOTE

This section exempts from stamp duty the disposals of land made by constituency associations as described in s **7**.

GIFTS INTER VIVOS

Stamp duty is chargeable under F(1909–10)A 1910 s **74** on the value of property which is the subject of a voluntary disposition inter vivos. However, such dispositions of land between either—

(*a*) existing associations and successor new associations directly, or

(*b*) existing associations and successor new associations via the medium of a body which is an organ of the political party concerned

are to be exempt from stamp duty.

CONVEYANCE CONSIDERATION OF A DEBT

Under the Stamp Act 1891 s **57**, where property is conveyed in whole or part consideration of a debt or subject to the payment or transfer of money or stock, the value or part of the value, chargeable with ad valorem stamp duty is taken as the value of the debt, money or stock. This provision will not apply to a disposition as exempted above.

DOCUMENTS DULY STAMPED

The Inland Revenue Commissioners may be required to express their opinion on any executed instrument as to whether—

(*a*) it is chargeable with duty and

(*b*) if so, with what amount of duty.

If they are satisfied that the instrument is not chargeable with duty, it should be stamped with a stamp denoting it is not chargeable (Stamp Act 1891 s 12).

An instrument which is only exempt from duty under F(1909–10)A s **74** by virtue of these provisions will not be regarded as duly stamped unless—

(*a*) it is stamped with a stamp indicating it is not chargeable, as under Stamp Act 1891 s 12, or

(*b*) it has been stamped with the duty with which it would have been chargeable but for these provisions.

For definitions of "existing association" etc and the types of disposal involved, refer to s **7** above.

16 Short title, construction and repeals

(1) This Act may be cited as the Finance (No 2) Act 1983.

(2) Part I of this Act, so far as it relates to income tax, shall be construed as one with the Income Tax Acts, so far as it relates to corporation tax, shall be construed as one with the Corporation Tax Acts and, so far as it relates to

capital gains tax, shall be construed as one with the Capital Gains Tax Act 1979.

(3) Part II of this Act shall be construed as one with Part III of the Finance Act 1975.

(4) The enactments specified in Schedule 2 to this Act are hereby repealed to the extent specified in the third column of that Schedule, but subject to any provision at the end of any Part of that Schedule.

SCHEDULES

SCHEDULE 1

Section 5

AMENDMENTS OF PART I OF SCHEDULE 5 TO THE FINANCE ACT 1983

1 Schedule **5** to the Finance Act **1983** shall be amended as follows.

2 In paragraph 4 (1) for the words "throughout the year of assessment in which" there shall be substituted the words "at the time when".

GENERAL NOTE

An individual investor is required by FA **1983** Sch **5** para 4(1) to be resident in the UK *throughout* the year of assessment in which the shares that are the subject of his claim are issued. This requirement is now relaxed so that he needs only to be resident *at the time when* they are issued. An individual who is deemed to become resident at some point in the year prior to the issue and an individual who is deemed to cease residence after the issue will not now be disqualified for that reason alone.

3 In paragraph 5—

(*a*) in sub-paragraph (2) (*b*) (ii) after the words "carrying on" there shall be inserted the words "wholly or mainly in the United Kingdom"; and

(*b*) after sub-paragraph (10) there shall be inserted the following sub-paragraph—

"(11) In sub-paragraphs (8) and (10) above references to a company's trade include references to the trade of any of its subsidiaries."

GENERAL NOTE

A qualifying company under the business expansion scheme may, throughout the period of three years from the date of issue of the relevant shares (or, if it is not then carrying on a qualifying trade of three years from the commencement of that trade) only carry on certain prescribed activities. It will be a qualifying company, if, inter alia, its business consists (FA 1983 Sch 5 para 5(2)(*b*)(ii)) wholly of both—

(*a*) holding shares or securities of, or making loans to, one or more qualifying subsidiaries and

(*b*) carrying on one or more qualifying trades.

The amendment made by para 3 (*a*) ensures that those qualifying trades must be carried on wholly or mainly in the UK. This removes the anomaly whereby if the company was a trading company, it was required to carry on the [qualifying] trade(s) wholly or mainly in the UK (FA 1983 Sch 5 para 5(2)(*a*)) but if it was a mixed trading and holding company, as above, there was no such requirement.

A company will not qualify if within a certain period (specified in para 10) and after 5 April 1983, an individual who has or has had control over a similar trade acquires a controlling interest in that company's trade (FA 1983 Sch 5 para 5 (8)). This prohibition is now extended to the trades of subsidiaries by the insertion of a new subparagraph (11) to para 5.

4—(1) Paragraph **7** shall be amended as follows.

(2) In sub-paragraph (2)—

(*a*) after the words "ordinary shares", where they first occur, there shall be inserted the words "of any class";

(*b*) after the word "some" there shall be inserted the words "shares of that class"; and

(*c*) after the words "ordinary shares", in the second place where they occur, there shall be inserted the words "of that class".

(3) After sub-paragraph (2) there shall be inserted the following sub-paragraph—

"(2A) Where the relief has been given to an individual in respect of shares of any class in a company which have been issued to him at different times, any disposal by him of shares of that class shall be treated for the purposes of this paragraph as relating to those issued earlier rather than to those issued later."

(4) In sub-paragraph (3) for the words from the beginning to "subsection (4)" there shall be substituted the words "Section **57** (4) of Chapter II shall apply but".

(5) After sub-paragraph (3) there shall be inserted the following sub-paragraph—

"(4) Shares in a company shall not be treated for the purposes of this paragraph as being of the same class unless they would be so treated if dealt with on The Stock Exchange."

GENERAL NOTE

FA **1983** Sch **5** para **7** provides for withdrawal of relief where shares are disposed of within the relevant period and contains rules for the identification of disposals.

The business expansion scheme unlike (originally) the start up scheme, allows for ordinary shares of different classes. The identification rules in para **7** were, however, to be those applying to the start up scheme (FA **1981** s **57** (3)) and consequently do not differentiate between ordinary shares of different classes. The amendments made by this paragraph ensure that the identification rules of para **7** apply as between shares of the same class only and hence remove the reference to s **57** (3). Shares of that class for which relief has been given will be treated as disposed of before non-relief shares of that class and as between relief shares of the same class, those issued earlier will be deemed disposed of before those issued later.

A new subparagraph (4) provides that, for the purposes of para **7** as amended, shares will be treated as being of the same class only if they satisfy the Stock Exchange requirements for that treatment.

5 In paragraph **8** (3) for the words from "connected" to "Chapter II)" there shall be substituted the words "who would, for the purposes of paragraph **4** above, be treated as connected with the company".

GENERAL NOTE

FA **1983** Sch **5** para **8** provides for relief to be withdrawn when an individual receives value from the company and specifies the occasions on which value is treated as being received. Para **8** (3) provides that an individual receives value when any person connected with the company purchases any share capital or securities belonging to the individual or makes any payment to him for giving up any rights in relation to the company's share capital or securities. "Connected" is defined by reference to FA **1981** s **54**. The amendment now made is to define "connected" by reference to FA **1983** Sch **5** para **4**, ie the business expansion scheme rules. Although para **4** itself applies the tests of s **54** (2)–(8) it provides that an overdraft the company may have with a bank, as long as it arose in the ordinary course of the bank's business, is not included as part of the company's loan capital for the purposes of those tests.

6 In paragraph **9**—

(*a*) in sub-paragraph (1) (*a*) (i) after the words "carry on" there shall be inserted the words "as its trade or as part of its trade" and for the words "by a person other than" there shall be substituted the words "otherwise than by";

(*b*) in sub-paragraph (2), in paragraphs (*a*) and (*b*), and in sub-paragraph (3)(*b*), for the words "the person or", in each case where they first occur, there shall be substituted the words "any person or group of";

(*c*) in sub-paragraph (2) (*a*)—

(i) for the words "the person or", in the second place where they occur, there shall be substituted the words "a person or group of"; and

(ii) for the words "(as transferred)" there shall be substituted the words "carried on by the company";

(*d*) in sub-paragraphs (2) (*b*) and (3) (*b*) for the words "are the person or" there shall be substituted the words "is or are a person or group of"; and (*e*) in sub-paragraph (5) for the words "and any part of a trade" there shall be substituted the words "; and references to a trade previously carried on include references to part of such a trade".

GENERAL NOTE

Relief is withdrawn or withheld where, in certain circumstances prescribed by FA 1983 Sch 5 para 9, an individual has the opportunity to receive back any of the capital he subscribed from someone other than the company.

One of the circumstances prescribed by paragraph 9 is that in which, at any time in the relevant period, the company or qualifying subsidiary—

(*a*) commences a trade previously carried on by a person other than the company or qualifying subsidiary or

(*b*) acquires the whole or the greater part of the assets used for the purposes of a trade so carried on and

(*c*) the person or persons controlling, or previously in control of, the company also control(s), or have controlled, another company that previously carried on the trade or

(*d*) the person or persons owning at least a half share in the trade before its transfer also own(s), or have owned, such a share in the trade as transferred.

Several amendments are now made to the wording of these provisions—

(*a*) the references to "a person or persons" are replaced by references to "any person or group of persons", thus ensuring that the persons in question have some common link;

(*b*) the reference to commencing "a trade" is particularised by adding the words "as its trade or as part of its trade", thus restricting the scope of the paragraph to a trade that the qualifying company or its subsidiary is carrying on as its qualifying trade or as part of its qualifying trade;

(*c*) the reference to a trade previously carried on by "a person other than" the company or a subsidiary is replaced by "otherwise than by" the company or a subsidiary: there appears to be no practical difference between the old and new wording;

(*d*) the words "as transferred" in paragraph (*d*) above are replaced by "carried on by the company", thus broadening the reference from the transferred trade to include the qualifying trade carried on by the company as a whole.

The definition of trade is altered so that only references to a trade previously carried on include references to part of such a trade for the purposes of paragraph 9.

7 In paragraph 10, after sub-paragraph (5) there shall be inserted the following sub-paragraph—

"(5A) Where, by virtue of section 59 (3) of Chapter II and sub-paragraph (5) above, any relief is withheld or withdrawn in the case of an individual to whom ordinary shares in the company have been issued at different times, the relief shall be withheld or withdrawn in respect of shares issued earlier rather than in respect of shares issued later."

GENERAL NOTE

FA 1983 Sch 5 para 10 provides for relief to be withdrawn from an individual when some other member of the company receives value from it. Where that individual held shares issued at different times, however, there was no identification rule to attribute the relief withdrawn to any particular shares. Such a rule, prescribing that relief should first be treated as withdrawn from shares issued earlier rather than later is now introduced.

8 In paragraph 14 (2) (*a*) after "6" there shall be inserted "9".

GENERAL NOTE

When relief is withdrawn, FA 1983 Sch 5 para 14 prescribes what is to be the reckonable date (TMA 1970 s 86) for the calculation of interest on overdue tax. No reference was made to relief withdrawn by virtue of para 9 (return of capital by someone other than the company to a qualifying individual). This omission is rectified and the reckonable date for para 9 is to be the date of the event giving rise to the withdrawal.

9 Paragraph 17 (1) (*c*), and in paragraph 18 (1) the words "within the next four months", shall be omitted.

GENERAL NOTE

A qualifying company is permitted to have subsidiaries if, broadly speaking, each of those subsidiaries would in its own right be a qualifying company. As prescribed by FA 1983 Sch 5 para 17, each subsidiary had, inter alia—

(*a*) to be incorporated in the UK and be a company which existed wholly, or substantially wholly (sic), for the purpose of carrying on one or more qualifying trades wholly or mainly in the UK (ie satisfy the requirements of FA 1983 Sch 5 para 5(2)(*a*)) *and*

(*b*) to comply with the requirement of para 5(2) as a whole, which entailed its being an unquoted company resident only in the UK and *either* a company falling within sub-para 2 (*a*) (as in (*a*) above) *or* falling within sub-para 2(*b*) (which would permit it to be a holding or finance company for subsidiaries).

This second requirement (para 17(1)(*c*)) thus not only duplicated para 17(1)(*b*) but was also contradictory in that whilst para 17(1)(*b*) required the subsidiary to be a trading company, para 17(1)(*c*) also allowed it to be wholly or partly a holding or finance company. This contradiction is removed by striking out para 17(1)(*c*). A further consequence of this is that there is now no requirement that the subsidiary be *resident* in the UK; it need only be incorporated in the UK and wholly or substantially carry on a qualifying trade or trades within the UK.

SUBSIDIARIES INTENDING TO CARRY ON A TRADE

One of the purposes for which a qualifying company may issue eligible shares under the scheme is to raise money for a qualifying trade which is being carried on by a subsidiary or which that subsidiary intends to carry on. As enacted, FA 1983 Sch 5 para 18 (1) requires the subsidiary in the latter case to intend commencing the trade within four months of the issue.

The four month requirement is now removed and the intention, without a fixed time within which to carry it out, is now sufficient. Relief will still not be allowed, by virtue of Sch 5 para 2 (4), if the subsidiary's qualifying trade has not commenced when the shares are issued, unless it does commence that trade within two years of the issue and then not until it has been trading for four months.

Section 16 (4)

SCHEDULE 2

REPEALS

PART I

INCOME TAX, CORPORATION TAX AND CAPITAL GAINS TAX

Chapter	Short title	Extent of repeal
1983 c 28	The Finance Act 1983	In section 10, in subsection (1), the words following "30 per cent" and subsections (2) and (3) Section 16 In Schedule 5, in paragraph 17 (1), paragraph (*c*) and the word "and" immediately preceding it and, in paragraph 18 (1), the words "within the next four months"

Part II
Capital Transfer Tax

Chapter	Short title	Extent of repeal
1925 c 23	The Administration of Estates Act 1925	In the First Schedule, paragraph 8 *(b)*
1955 c 24 (NI)	The Administration of Estates Act (Northern Ireland) 1955	In the First Schedule, paragraph 8 (*b*)
1975 c 7	The Finance Act 1975	In section 26 (3), the words "10 (1) (*b*) or", "given to a charity or property" and "charity or, as the case may be, the" In section 45, in subsection (1), paragraph (*c*) and the word "or" immediately preceding it, and subsections (2A) and (3) In Schedule 4, in paragraphs 12 (3) and 19 (2), the words "a charity or only" In Schedule 6, in paragraph 10 (1), paragraph (*b*) and the word "and" immediately preceding it
1976 c 40	The Finance Act 1976	In Schedule 10, paragraph 2 (1A) (*b*)
1977 c 36	The Finance Act 1977	Section 49
1982 c 39	The Finance Act 1982	Section 92 (2)

1 The repeals in the Administration of Estates Act 1925 and the Administration of Estates Act (Northern Ireland) 1955 have effect in relation to deaths on or after the day on which this Act is passed.

2 The repeals of—

(*a*) subsections (1) (*c*), (2A) and (3) of section 45 of the Finance Act 1975,

(*b*) paragraph 2 (1A) (*b*) of Schedule 10 to the Finance Act 1976, and

(*c*) section 49 of the Finance Act 1977,

have effect in relation to transfers of value made, and other events occurring, on or after 15th March 1983.

3 The remaining repeals have effect in relation to transfers of value made on or after 15th March 1983.

INDEX

References are to F(No 2)A 1983

Printed by the Whitefriars Press Ltd, Tonbridge